The Corporate Income Tax System: Overview and Options for Reform

Mark P. Keightley
Specialist in Economics

Molly F. Sherlock
Specialist in Public Finance

September 13, 2012

Congressional Research Service
7-5700
www.crs.gov
R42726

CRS Report for Congress
Prepared for Members and Committees of Congress

Summary

Many economists and policymakers believe that the U.S. corporate tax system is in need of reform. There is, however, disagreement over why the corporate tax system needs to be reformed, and what specific policy measures should be included in a reform. To assist policymakers in designing and evaluating corporate tax proposals, this report (1) briefly reviews the current U.S. corporate tax system; (2) discusses economic factors that may be considered in the corporate tax reform debate; and (3) presents corporate tax reform policy options, including a brief discussion of current corporate tax reform proposals.

The current U.S. corporate income tax system generally taxes corporate income at a rate of 35%. This tax is applied to income earned domestically and abroad, although taxes on certain income earned abroad can be deferred indefinitely if that income remains overseas. The U.S. corporate tax system also contains a number of deductions, exemptions, deferrals, and tax credits, often referred to as "tax expenditures." Collectively, these provisions reduce the effective tax rate paid by many U.S. corporations below the 35% statutory rate. In 2011, the sum of all corporate tax expenditures was $158.8 billion.

The significance of the corporate tax as a federal revenue source has declined over time. At its post-WWII peak in 1952, the corporate tax generated 32.1% of all federal tax revenue. In 2010, the corporate tax accounted for 8.9% of federal tax revenue. The decline in corporate revenues is a combination of decreasing effective tax rates, an increasing fraction of business activity that is being carried out by pass-through entities (particularly partnerships and S corporations, which are not subject to the corporate tax), and a decline in corporate sector profitability.

A particular aspect of the corporate tax system that receives substantial attention is the 35% statutory corporate tax rate. Although the U.S. has the world's highest statutory corporate tax rate, the U.S. effective corporate tax rate is similar to the Organization for Economic Co-operation and Development (OECD) average. Further, the U.S. collects less in corporate tax revenue relative to Gross Domestic Production (GDP) (1.9% in 2009) than the average of other OECD countries (2.8% in 2009).

This report discusses a number of economic considerations that may be made while evaluating various corporate tax reform proposals. These might include analyses of the likely effect on households of certain reforms (also known as incidence analysis). Policymakers might also want to consider how certain corporate tax provisions contribute to the allocation of economic resources, choosing policies that promote an efficient use of resources. Other goals of corporate tax reform may include designing a system that is simple to comply with and administer, while also promoting competitiveness of U.S. corporations.

Commonly discussed corporate tax reforms include policies that would broaden the tax base (i.e., eliminate tax expenditures) to finance reduced corporate tax rates. Concerns that the U.S. corporate tax system inefficiently imposes a "double tax" on corporate income has led some to consider an integration of the corporate and individual tax systems. The treatment of pass-through income—business income not earned by C corporations—has also received considerable attention in tax reform debates. How the U.S. taxes income earned abroad, and the possibility of moving to a territorial tax system, have emerged as important issues. Both the Obama Administration and the House Committee on Ways and Means Chairman David Camp have released tax reform proposals that would change the current tax treatment of U.S. multinationals.

Contents

Structure of the Corporate Income Tax 1
    Corporate Tax Rates 2
    Corporate Tax Expenditures 3
    Treatment of Losses 5
    Corporate Income Earned Abroad 6
    Taxation of Shareholders 6
Which Companies Pay? 7
Corporate Income Tax Revenues 11
International Comparisons 12
    Tax Rates 12
    Tax Revenues 13
Economic Considerations 15
    Why Have a Corporate Income Tax? 15
    Corporate Tax Incidence 16
    Evaluating the Corporate Income Tax 17
        Equity 17
        Efficiency 19
        Simplicity and Administrability 22
Options for Reform 23
    Broader Base, Lower Rates 23
    Integration of the Corporate and Individual Tax Systems 25
        Other Options for Reducing "Double Taxation" of Corporate Income 26
    Taxation of Pass-Through Income 26
    International Tax: Territorial vs. Worldwide Taxation 27
Comparing Current Corporate and Business Tax Reform Proposals 28

Figures

Figure 1. Individual and Corporate Tax Expenditures in FY2011 4
Figure 2. Distribution of Business Types, 1980 and 2008 8
Figure 3. Distribution of Corporations and Corporate Taxes Paid in 2008 by Industry 9
Figure 4. Corporate Tax Revenue as a Percentage of GDP, 1946-2010 12
Figure 5. Corporate Tax Revenue as a Percentage of GDP in 2009 14

Tables

Table 1. Ten Largest Corporate Tax Expenditures in FY2011 5
Table 2. Corporate Tax Rates: Comparing the United States to the Rest of the OECD 13
Table 3. CBO's Distribution of Corporate Income Tax 18
Table 4. Treasury's Distribution of Corporate Income Tax 19

Table 5. Comparing Business and Corporate Tax Reform Proposals 31

Contacts

Author Contact Information.. 34

The corporate income tax system has been a focus of many recent debates about tax reform and the economy. Many economists and policymakers argue that reform of the corporate income tax system is needed, although a variety of rationales on why and how have been offered. Some argue that a simpler system with lower tax rates is necessary to encourage domestic investment, employment, and economic growth. Others argue that reform is needed to close loopholes and restrict access to tax havens, both of which are seen by some to allow corporations to avoid taxes too easily. A number of others have advocated for corporate tax reform on the basis that the current system puts American corporations at a disadvantage when compared with foreign competitors. Many believe it is a combination of these arguments that justify reforming the corporate tax system.

This report presents information and research on the corporate tax to help policymakers understand and evaluate arguments presented in the tax reform debate. Many of the topics and ideas discussed here are analyzed in greater detail in the other CRS reports and academic research referenced throughout. This report first reviews the structure of the corporate income tax. Data on which companies pay the corporate tax, corporate tax revenue, and how the U.S. system compares to the rest of the world is then presented and analyzed. Next, the economic effects of the corporate tax are reviewed—including a discussion of the purpose of the corporate tax, who bears the burden of the tax, and how to evaluate alternative corporate tax systems. The report then reviews broad reform options and concludes with a comparison of specific proposals that have been offered.

Structure of the Corporate Income Tax

The corporate income tax generally only applies to C corporations (also known as regular corporations). These corporations—named for Subchapter C of the Internal Revenue Code (IRC), which details their tax treatment—are generally treated as taxable entities separate from their shareholders.[1] That is, corporate income is taxed once at the corporate level according to the corporate income tax system. When corporate dividend payments are made or capital gains are realized income is taxed again at the individual-shareholder level according to the individual tax system. This treatment leads to the so-called "double taxation" of corporate profits. In contrast, non-corporate businesses, including S corporations[2] and partnerships,[3] pass their income through to owners who pay taxes. Collectively, these non-corporate business entities are referred to as

---

[1] For more information, see CRS Report R40748, *Business Organizational Choices: Taxation and Responses to Legislative Changes*, by Mark P. Keightley.

[2] An S corporation is a closely held corporation that elects to be treated as a pass-through entity for tax purposes. S corporations are named for Subchapter S of the IRC, which details their tax treatment. By electing S corporation status, a business is able to combine many of the legal and business advantages of a C corporation with the tax advantages of a partnership. For more information, see CRS Report R40748, *Business Organizational Choices: Taxation and Responses to Legislative Changes*, by Mark P. Keightley.

[3] A partnership is a joint venture consisting of at least two partners organized to operate a trade or business with each partner sharing profits, losses, deductions, credits, and the like. A partner is an investor in such an entity and may be an individual, a trust, a partnership, a corporation, another entity (such as a limited liability company), or a broker that is holding the ownership interest of an unnamed partner. Partnerships are established under the individual laws of each state, although their tax treatment at the federal level is determined by the Internal Revenue Code (IRC). The most common partnerships include general partnerships, limited liability partnerships, limited partnerships, publicly traded partnerships, and electing large partnerships. For more information, see CRS Report R40748, *Business Organizational Choices: Taxation and Responses to Legislative Changes*, by Mark P. Keightley.

pass-throughs. For these types of entities, business income is taxed only once, at individual income tax rates.

The corporate income tax is designed as a tax on corporate profits (also known as net income). Broadly defined, corporate profit is total income minus the cost associated with generating that income.[4] Business expenses that may be deducted from income include employee compensation; the decline in value of machines, equipment, and structures (i.e., deprecation); general supplies and materials; advertising; and interest payments. The corporate income tax also allows for a number of other special deductions, credits, and tax preferences. Oftentimes, these provisions are intended to promote particular policy goals, as deductions reduce taxes paid by corporations.

A corporation's tax liability can be calculated as:

$$\text{Taxes} = [(\text{Total Income} - \text{Expenses})(1 - p) \times t] - \text{Tax Credits},$$

where t is the statutory tax rate and p is the Section 199 production activities deduction. The Section 199 deduction, which is discussed in "Corporate Tax Expenditures" section, effectively lowers the corporate tax rate for those corporations engaged in domestic manufacturing activities.[5]

The corporate tax system becomes increasingly complex as the details of specific provisions are examined. The following sections discuss some of the more fundamental features of the tax system.

Corporate Tax Rates

Most corporate income is subject to a 35% statutory tax rate. To generate this flat rate, which applies to the largest businesses, income is taxed at rates that vary from 15% on the first $50,000 of income to 35% on income over $18,333,333.[6] This rate structure benefits smaller corporations, encouraging some small firms to incorporate to take advantage of scenarios where paying corporate taxes is less costly than paying according to the individual tax system.[7]

The corporate tax rate increases above 35% for two income brackets. Corporations with taxable income between $100,000 and $335,000 are subject to a 39% tax rate, and corporations with income between $15,000,000 and $18,333,333 are subject to a 38% tax rate. These "bubble" brackets increase the effective tax rate for higher-income corporations by offsetting any tax savings they would realize from having the first $75,000 in income taxed at lower rates.

---

[4] The primary components of business income are revenues generated from the sale of goods and services. Other income sources include investment income, royalties, rents, and capital gains.

[5] For more information on the production activities deduction, see CRS Report R41988, *The Section 199 Production Activities Deduction: Background and Analysis*, by Molly F. Sherlock.

[6] Corporations providing services in the fields of health care, law, engineering, architecture, accounting, actuarial science, the performing arts, and consulting are taxed at a fixed rate of 35%, regardless of their amount of taxable income. Internal Revenue Code (IRC) § 11(b)(2) denies personal service corporations the benefits of corporate graduated rates.

[7] For more information on benefits for small businesses in the corporate tax system, see CRS Report RL32254, *Small Business Tax Benefits: Current Law and Economic Justification*, by Gary Guenther.

One of the main points of contention in the debate over the corporate tax is that the 35% tax rate is too high. This rate is the *statutory* federal tax rate, defined as the legally imposed rate on taxable income. But this rate alone does not determine how much corporations pay in taxes. Because of a number of business tax benefits (deductions, credits, exemptions, etc.) in the corporate tax system, the *effective* (or actual) tax rate paid by corporations is typically less than the statutory rate. These tax benefits, known as tax expenditures, are discussed in the next section.

It is also important to understand that effective tax rates can vary substantially among U.S. corporations and across corporations in the same industry. For example, some corporations rely more on debt financing, which is treated more favorably than equity financing in the tax code. Those corporations that rely on tax-preferred financing reduce their effective tax rate relative to those who do not. Some corporations and industries rely more on certain physical assets that can be depreciated ("written-off") more quickly than investments made by companies in others industries, which again leads to differing effective tax rates. Other corporations and industries have more extensive overseas operations, which may affect their effective U.S. tax rate.

Corporate Tax Expenditures

The corporate tax system contains a variety of incentives designed to encourage certain types of behaviors and assist certain businesses. These incentives are formally known as corporate tax expenditures and include special credits, deductions, exemptions, exclusions, and tax rates that result in revenue loss for the federal government.[8] Some of the largest corporate tax expenditures include accelerated depreciation, the domestic production activities deduction (Section 199 deduction), and the deferral of income earned abroad. Tax expenditures are not exclusive to the corporate tax system. In fact, individual tax expenditures result in nearly 10 times the revenue loss to the federal government (see **Figure 1**) relative to corporate tax expenditures.

---

[8] The Budget Control Act of 1974 (P.L. 93-344) officially defines a tax expenditure as "revenue losses attributable to provisions of the Federal tax laws which allow a special exclusion, exemption, or deduction from gross income or which provide a special credit, a preferential rate of tax, or a deferral of tax liability." The Joint Committee on Taxation (JCT) produces an estimate of the all individual and corporate tax expenditures each year. The latest tax expenditure estimates are available at http://www.jct.gov/.

Figure 1. Individual and Corporate Tax Expenditures in FY2011

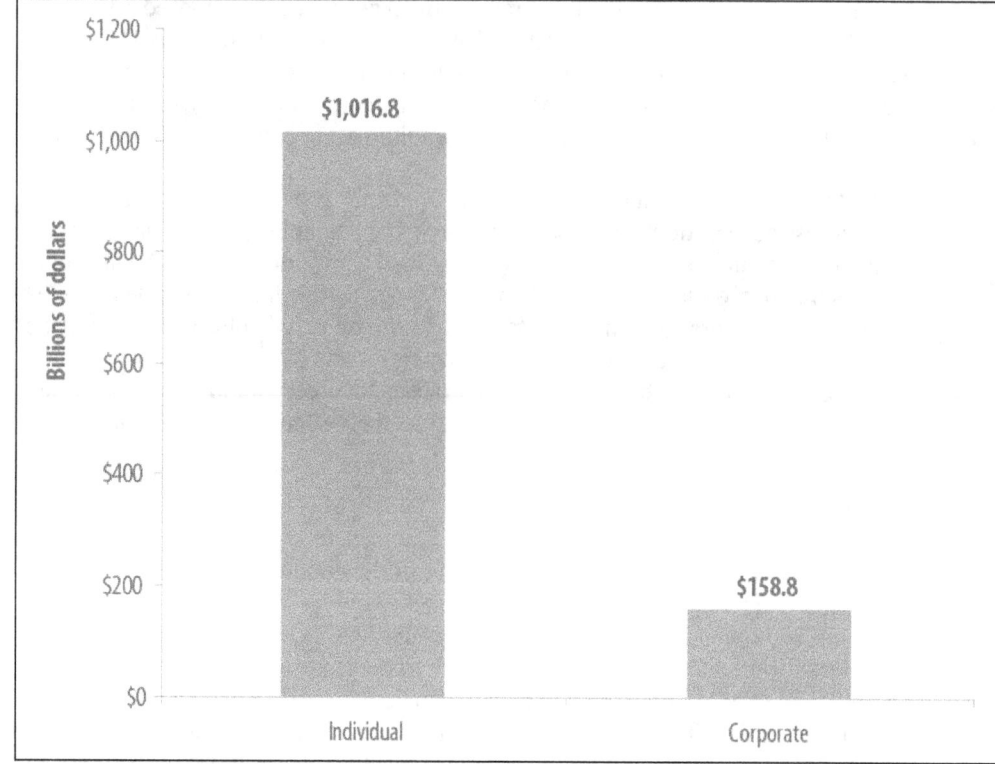

Source: CRS calculations using estimates in U.S. Congress, Joint Committee on Taxation, *Estimates of Federal Tax Expenditures for Fiscal Years 2011 - 2015*, committee print, prepared by Joint Committee on Taxation, 112th Cong., January 17, 2012, JCS-1-12.

In 2011, the sum of all corporate tax expenditures was $158.8 billion.[9] **Table 1** provides information on the ten largest corporate tax expenditure provisions in 2011, ranked according to projected revenue cost. Roughly 75% of the value (cost) of all corporate tax expenditures is attributable to these ten provisions. In 2011, roughly one-third ($52.3 billion) of the revenue cost of all corporate tax expenditures was due to provisions that allow for accelerated or bonus depreciation.[10] Bonus depreciation, a temporary provision to stimulate investment, is scheduled to expire at the end of 2012. Estimates suggest that by 2014, with the effects of bonus depreciation eliminated, depreciation provisions will cost roughly $35 billion.[11] Thus, the total value of corporate tax expenditures in 2011 is not a good measure of the long-run revenue potential from eliminating corporate tax expenditure provisions.

---

[9] The sum of all corporate tax expenditures is calculated using the estimates provided in U.S. Congress, Joint Committee on Taxation, *Estimates of Federal Tax Expenditures for Fiscal Years 2011 - 2015*, committee print, prepared by Joint Committee on Taxation, 112th Cong., January 17, 2012, JCS-1-12.

[10] For background, see CRS Report RL31852, *Section 179 and Bonus Depreciation Expensing Allowances: Current Law, Legislative Proposals in the 112th Congress, and Economic Effects*, by Gary Guenther.

[11] See Testimony of Jane G. Gravelle, Senate Committee on Finance, *Tax Reform Options: Incentives for Capital Investment and Manufacturing*, March 6, 2012, http://www.finance.senate.gov/imo/media/doc/Testimony%20of%20Jane%20Gravelle.pdf.

Table 1. Ten Largest Corporate Tax Expenditures in FY2011
billions of dollars

Corporate Tax Expenditure	Estimated Revenue Loss in 2011	Share of All Corporate Tax Expenditures	Cumulative Share of Corporate Tax Expenditures
Depreciation of Equipment in Excess of the Alternative Depreciation System	52.3	32.9%	32.9%
Deferral of Active Income of Controlled Foreign Corporations	15.3	9.6%	42.6%
Deduction for Income Attributable to Domestic Production Activities	8.9	5.6%	48.2%
Exclusion of Interest on Public Purpose State and Local Government Bonds	8.5	5.4%	53.5%
Inclusion of Income Arising from Business Indebtedness Discharged by the Reacquision of a Debt Instrument	6.9	4.3%	57.9%
Deferral of Active Financing Income	6.2	3.9%	61.8%
Inventory Property Sales Source Rule Exception	6.0	3.8%	65.6%
Credit for Increasing Research Activities	5.8	3.7%	69.2%
Credit for Low-Income Housing	5.1	3.2%	72.4%
Expensing of Research and Experimental Expenditures	4.1	2.6%	75.0%
All other Corporate Tax Expenditures	39.7	25.0%	100%%
Total	**158.8**	**100%**	**100%**

Source: CRS analysis using data from U.S. Congress, Joint Committee on Taxation, *Estimates of Federal Tax Expenditures for Fiscal Years 2011 - 2015*, committee print, prepared by Joint Committee on Taxation, 112th Cong., January 17, 2012, JCS-1-12.

Notes: The sum of individual tax expenditure estimates may not equal the total value of tax expenditures because of interaction effects. Tax expenditure estimates are projections of foregone revenue (or revenue cost) associated with various tax provisions and thus do not reflect actual revenue loss.

Treatment of Losses

Another important component of the corporate tax system is the treatment of losses. A corporation that loses money in a particular year experiences what is known as a net operating loss (NOL).[12] No corporate tax is due when a company has a NOL because they do not have profits (e.g., total income less expenses is negative). In addition, a NOL can be "carried back" and deducted from up to two prior years' taxable income. The corporation is then eligible for a refund equal to the difference between previously paid taxes and taxes owed after deducting the current

---

[12] For more information on the tax treatment of corporate losses, see CRS Report RL34535, *Tax Treatment of Net Operating Losses*, by Mark P. Keightley.

year's loss. If the loss is too large to be fully carried back, it may be "carried forward" for up to 20 years and used to reduce future tax liabilities.

Allowing for the carryback of losses reduces the distorting effects of taxation on investment and, in turn, increases economic efficiency.[13] The government, by allowing NOL carrybacks, effectively enters into a partnership with taxpayers, sharing both the return to investment (tax revenue) and the risk of investment (revenue loss). When corporations earn income, they pay taxes. However, when corporations have losses, past and future tax liabilities are reduced through loss carrybacks, reducing risk. The further back losses can be carried, the closer is the taxpayer-government partnership, and the less distorting taxation becomes on investment.[14] Further gains in economic efficiency are possible if the government can spread risk better than can be done in private markets. Additionally, the ability to carry back losses helps to prevent two firms that earn the same amount over a given time period, but differ in the timing of when the income is earned, from paying different amounts in taxes.[15]

Corporate Income Earned Abroad

The taxation of American corporations with overseas operations is another important part of the corporate tax. The U.S. taxes American corporations on their worldwide income.[16] This approach to taxation is referred to as a worldwide (or resident-based) tax system. In contrast, a territorial (or source-based) system would tax American corporations only on income earned within the physical borders of the United States. In reality, no country has a pure worldwide or a pure territorial tax system.

Under current law, corporations are allowed a credit, known as the foreign tax credit, for taxes paid to other countries.[17] The foreign tax credit may not reduce a corporation's tax liability below zero. Additionally, corporations are not required to pay U.S. tax on overseas income until income is repatriated to the United States. This ability to defer taxes is often known simply as "deferral." Deferral is not an option, however, with "Subpart F" income, which generally includes passive types of income such as interest, dividends, annuities, rents, and royalties.[18]

Taxation of Shareholders

The after-tax profits of a corporation are typically subject to tax again when shareholders receive dividend distributions. Under current law, the tax rate on dividends is either 0% or 15%

---

[13] Evsey D. Domar and Richard A. Musgrave, "Proportional Income Taxation and Risk-Taking," *The Quarterly Journal of Economics*, vol. 58, May 1944, p. 388.

[14] For further discussion, see CRS Report RL34535, *Tax Treatment of Net Operating Losses*, by Mark P. Keightley.

[15] See Appendix A in the following report for a numerical example CRS Report RL34535, *Tax Treatment of Net Operating Losses*, by Mark P. Keightley.

[16] The concepts discussed here are described in greater detail in CRS Report R41852, *U.S. International Corporate Taxation: Basic Concepts and Policy Issues*, by Mark P. Keightley, and CRS Report RL34115, *Reform of U.S. International Taxation: Alternatives*, by Jane G. Gravelle.

[17] See IRC § 901.

[18] Subpart F income is named after the section of the Internal Revenue Code where its tax treatment is defined. An exception to Subpart F income is for "active financing" income. Active financing income is income earned by American corporations that operate banking, financing, and insurance lines of business abroad and is eligible for deferral.

depending on a taxpayer's ordinary income tax rate.[19] Taxpayers with an ordinary income tax rate of 15% or less pay the 0% rate on dividends, and taxpayers with an ordinary income tax rate greater than 15% pay the 15% dividend rate.[20] Barring congressional action, dividends are scheduled to be taxed at ordinary income tax rates (varying from 15% to 39.6%) after 2012. The rates currently in place were first enacted by the Jobs and Growth Tax Relief Reconciliation Act of 2003 (P.L. 108-27) and later extended by Tax Increase Prevention and Reconciliation Act of 2005 (P.L. 109-222), and the Tax Relief, Unemployment Insurance Reauthorization, and Job Creation Act of 2010 (P.L. 111-312).

Shareholders must also pay taxes on any capital gains they realize from selling shares that have appreciated in value.[21] The tax rate on the gain from investments held less than a year (short-term capital gains) is equal to the taxpayer's ordinary income tax rate. Gain from investments held longer than a year (long-term capital gains) is same as for dividends—either 0% or 15%—depending on whether the shareholder's ordinary income tax rate is above or below 15%. The same laws that put in place and later extended the dividend tax rates also established and extended the current capital gains rates (P.L. 108-27; P.L. 109-222; and P.L. 111-312).

Which Companies Pay?

Currently, about 6% of businesses are organized as C corporations, and thus subject to the corporate income tax. As **Figure 2** shows, this change is a significant decrease from the 17% of businesses that choose the corporate form in 1980. Some of this shift can be explained by various legislative and regulatory changes over this time period that reduced the top individual tax rate below the top corporate tax rate (making it more attractive to be a pass-through), increases in the shareholder limit for S corporations, and the ability of LLCs to elect partnership tax status.[22]

The share of business income generated by C corporations has also changed over time. In 1980, for example, corporations were responsible for nearly 80% of total business income. Today, corporations generate less than half of total business income, with the remainder coming from pass-throughs.[23] C corporations, however, still generate a disproportionate share of all business income.

---

[19] For information on current and historical individual income tax rates, including dividend tax rates, see CRS Report RL34498, *Statutory Individual Income Tax Rates and Other Key Elements of the Individual Income Tax: 1988 Through 2012*, by Gary Guenther.

[20] For more information, see CRS Report R41394, *Tax Treatment of Long-Term Capital Gains and Dividends and Related Provisions in the President's FY2011 Budget Proposal*, by Mark P. Keightley.

[21] Capital gains are earned through the sale of capital assets. Capital assets include real estate, household furnishings, and stocks or bonds. A capital gain (or loss) is the difference between the sales price of an assets and the asset's basis, which is generally the asset's cost. For more information, see Internal Revenue Service Topic 409 – Capital Gains and Losses, available at http://www.irs.gov/taxtopics/tc409.html.

[22] For a more detailed analysis of this shift see, CRS Report R40748, *Business Organizational Choices: Taxation and Responses to Legislative Changes*, by Mark P. Keightley.

[23] The exact figure has fluctuated over time and is sensitive to swings in the business cycle. For example, C corporations generated 27% of business income in 2009 (a recession year), and 54% in 2005. CRS calculations using the Internal Revenue Service Integrated Business Data, Table 1, http://www.irs.gov/pub/irs-soi/80ot1all.xls. Net income is measured as net income less deficit. Regulated investment companies (RICs) and real estate investment trust (REIT) were excluded.

Although C corporations only account for 6% of all businesses, they generate a disproportionate share of business income. But just as the fraction of businesses choosing the corporate form has decreased over time, so too has the fraction of income they generate.

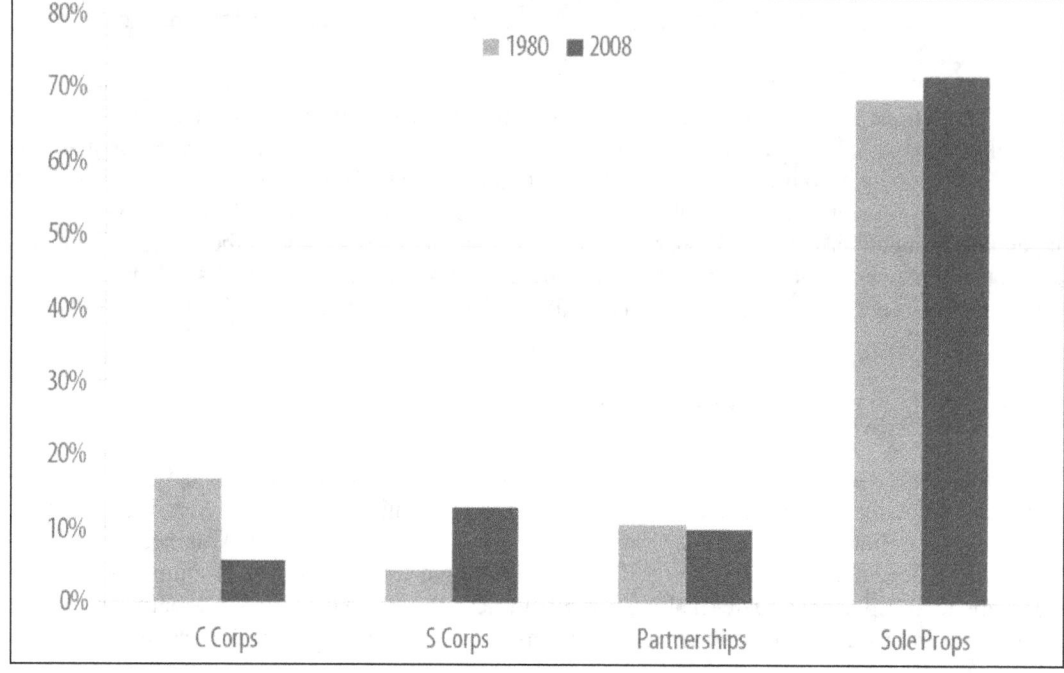

Figure 2. Distribution of Business Types, 1980 and 2008

Source: CRS calculations from Internal Revenue Service's Integrated Business Data

When looking at an industry level breakdown of what types of firms pay the corporate tax, manufacturing ranks number one (see **Figure 3**). In 2008, manufacturing was responsible for about 32% of corporate taxes paid. The wholesale and retail trade industry was next, accounting for 17% of corporate taxes paid, followed by the finance and insurance industry, which paid 16% of corporate taxes. The share paid by all other industries then drops sharply—8% paid by holding companies and the information industry, 4% by mining firms, and then no industry type accounted for more than 3% of taxes paid.

This distribution of taxes paid is partly explained by the fact that most corporate business activity is conducted by a rather small number of large firms. This distribution is evident from a comparison of the distribution of taxes paid to the distribution of corporations across industry (see **Figure 3**). For example, while manufacturing paid 32.3% of taxes, it only accounted for 6.1% of corporations. Similarly, the finance and insurance industry paid 16.0% of taxes, but contained 4.3% of all corporations. In total, the five industries that paid the most in taxes (80.9% combined) only accounted for 33% of corporations. Only the wholesale and retail trade industry paid taxes in proportion to their share of corporate firms.

Figure 3. Distribution of Corporations and Corporate Taxes Paid in 2008 by Industry

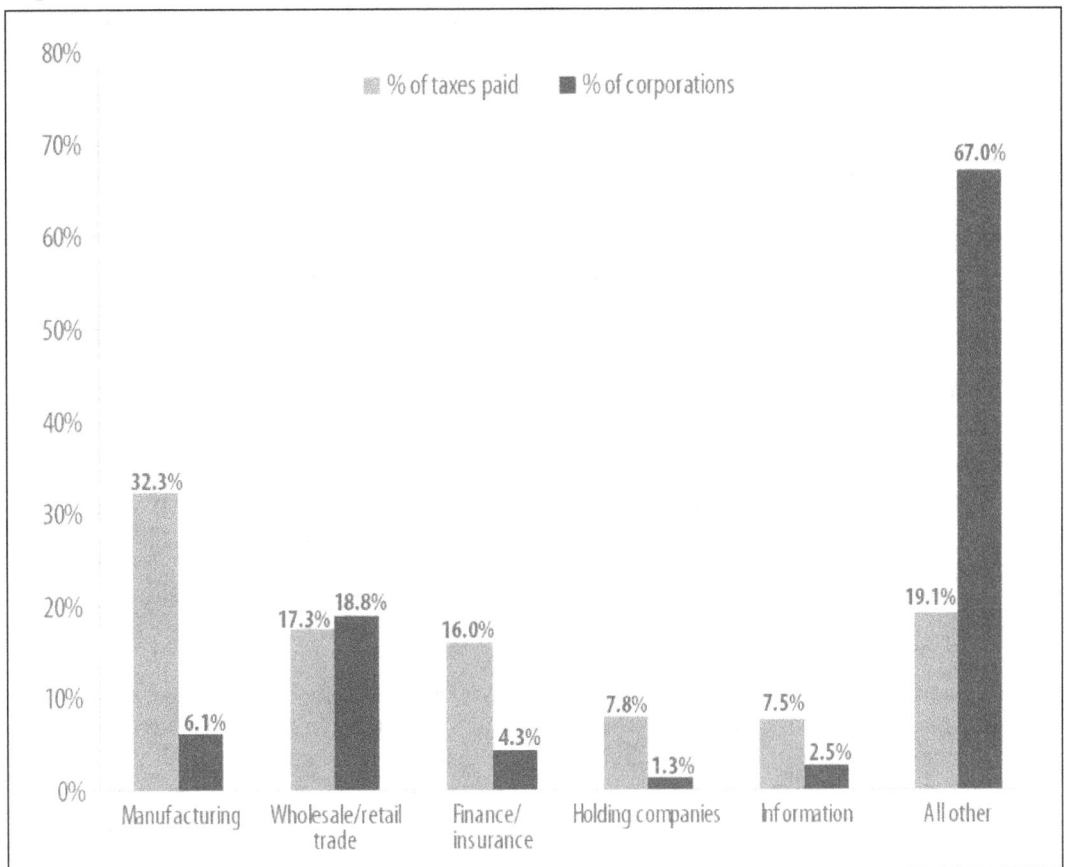

Source: CRS calculations from Internal Revenue Service's Statistics of Income, http://www.irs.gov/pub/irs-soi/08co21ccr.xls. Taxes paid are measured as "Total income tax after credits."

Notes: Data from 2005 display a similar distribution.

There is also substantial variation in taxes paid by corporations in different industries. One way to compare the tax burden across industries is to look at various measures of an effective tax rate. The ratio of taxes paid divided by profits is known simply as the "effective rate." The effective rate incorporates various tax benefits and subsidies that reduce the taxable income base relative to financial profits, and hence reduce the tax rate firms actually incur relative to the statutory rate. The "effective marginal tax rate" is the rate of taxation on a projected investment project: it is an estimate of how much the return on an investment will be paid in taxes. The effective marginal rate is arguably the most well suited measure for determining the effect of tax rates on investment decisions.

Data compiled by Aswath Damodaran, professor of finance at New York University, has been used to look at effective tax rates for U.S. companies across industrial sectors.[24] Damodaran's data set includes financial information from roughly 6,000 U.S. public companies. Effective tax rates are calculated as taxes paid divided by taxable income (in the basic calculations, companies

---

[24] This data is available online at http://pages.stern.nyu.edu/~adamodar/New_Home_Page/data.html.

reporting losses that pay no taxes are considered to have an effective tax rate of zero).[25] Industries with low effective tax rates tend to be those that are more likely to make large investments or expenditures on research and development (activities that are rewarded in the tax code). Examples include the biotechnology and semiconductor industries. Industries that tend have higher than average effective tax rates include retail, food services, and utilities.[26]

Research has also shown that, in recent years, effective tax rates reported to shareholders on earnings statements by the most profitable U.S. companies has declined.[27] This decline has occurred despite the fact that the statutory corporate tax rate has remained constant at 35%. The decline in effective tax rates for large U.S. corporations over time can largely be explained by increased international activity, combined with lower foreign tax rates. Tax expenditures have played a limited role in this change.

Economists oftentimes use an effective tax rate to evaluate how the tax system affects incentives for capital investment. The effective marginal tax rate, which measures the impact of the tax system on investment decisions, can be defined as $(\rho - r)/\rho$, where ρ is the real before-tax return on the marginal (or incremental) investment and r is the real return paid to investors.[28] Higher effective marginal tax rates indicate greater potential investment distortions. Negative effective tax rates indicate that the tax code is actually subsidizing investment to the point where taxpayers are willing to accept a before-tax rate of return that is less than the after-tax rate of return for an investment.[29]

There are a number of factors that contribute to differences in effective marginal tax rates. These factors include the form of business organization, financing method (e.g., debt versus equity), whether a particular industry is more capital intensive than others, inflation, etc.[30] Tax expenditure provisions also contribute to variation in effective marginal tax rates. A 2005 Congressional Budget Office (CBO) study calculating effective marginal tax rates for different asset types in the corporate sector found an overall effective marginal tax rate of 26.3%.[31]

---

[25] For more on Damodaran's effective tax rate calculations, see http://aswathdamodaran.blogspot.com/2011/01/tax-policy.html.

[26] Base broadening, rate reducing corporate tax reforms will likely change effective tax rates faced by different industries. If all tax expenditures were eliminated to reduce corporate tax rates, industries that currently have low effective tax rates due to tax expenditures could experience increased tax burdens. For further discussion, see the section "Broader Base, Lower Rates" below.

[27] Martin Sullivan, *Corporate Tax Reform: Taxing Profits in the 21st Century* (New York, NY: Apress, 2011).

[28] Assume, for example, that investors require an after-tax rate of return of 6% on a given investment. Assume next that a project must have a real before-tax rate of return of 9% to cover taxes, depreciation, and payments to investors. Under these conditions, the effective tax rate would be 33%.

[29] For more on this method of computing effective tax rates, see Congressional Budget Office, *Computing Effective Tax Rates on Capital Income*, Background Paper, Washington, DC, December 2006, https://www.cbo.gov/publication/18259.

[30] Changes in the tax code have contributed to fluctuations in effective marginal tax rates on capital income over time. For more information, see CRS Report RS21706, *Historical Effective Marginal Tax Rates on Capital Income*, by Jane G. Gravelle.

[31] Congressional Budget Office, *Taxing Capital Income: Effective Rates and Approaches to Reform*, Washington, DC, October 2005, http://www.cbo.gov/publication/17393. More detail on CBO's effective tax rate calculations is available at https://www.cbo.gov/publication/18259.

Gravelle (2011) also calculates effective tax rates by asset type, finding an average effective tax rate of 30%.[32]

Both the 2005 CBO study and Gravelle (2011) identified the computers and peripheral equipment, automobile equipment, and industrial and commercial building sectors as being highly taxed—facing effective marginal tax rates of 30% or above. Assets with the lowest effective marginal tax rates—less than 20% in both studies—were communications equipment, ships and boats, railroad equipment, mining structures, and petroleum and natural gas structures.

Corporate Income Tax Revenues

Corporate tax revenues have been declining over the last six decades. The corporate tax reached its post-World War II era peak in 1952 at 6.1% of gross domestic product (GDP) (see **Figure 4**). In 2010, the corporate tax generated revenue equal to approximately 1.3% of GDP. The corporate tax has also decreased in significance relative to other revenue sources. At its post-WWII peak in 1952, the corporate tax generated 32.1% of all federal tax revenue. In that same year the individual tax accounted for 42.2% of federal revenue, and the payroll tax accounted for 9.7% of revenue.[33] In 2010, the corporate tax accounted for 8.9% of federal tax revenue, whereas the individual and payroll taxes generated 41.5% and 40.0%, respectively, of federal revenue.

There are several factors that help explain the declining significance of the corporate tax.[34] First, the average effective corporate tax rate has decreased over time, mostly as a result of reductions in the statutory rate and changes affecting the tax treatment of investment and capital recovery (depreciation). Second, the increasing fraction of business activity that is being carried out by pass-throughs (particularly partnerships and S corporations) has lead to an erosion of the corporate tax base. Third, corporate-sector profitability has fallen over time, leading to a further erosion of the corporate tax base. Declining corporate sector profitability may be a result of several factors, including a shift within the corporate sector from less volatile to more volatile industries, a shift in the age of corporations from older to younger, and shifting of profits out of the United States and into lower-tax countries.[35]

---

[32] Jane G. Gravelle, "Reducing Depreciation Allowances to Finance a Lower Corporate Tax Rate," *National Tax Journal*, vol. 64, no. 4 (2011), pp. 1039-1054.

[33] For more information on the various components of the U.S. tax system, see CRS Report RL32808, *Overview of the Federal Tax System*, by Molly F. Sherlock and Donald J. Marples.

[34] For a more detailed analysis of declining corporate tax revenues, see CRS Report R42113, *Reasons for the Decline in Corporate Tax Revenues*, by Mark P. Keightley.

[35] For more on the effects on international profit shifting see, CRS Report R40623, *Tax Havens: International Tax Avoidance and Evasion*, by Jane G. Gravelle; Kimberly A. Clausing, "The Revenue Effects of Multinational Firm Income Shifting," Tax Notes, March 28, 2011, pp. 1580-1586; Kimberly A. Clausing, "Multinational Firm Tax Avoidance and Tax Policy," National Tax Journal , vol. 62 (December 2009), pp. 703-725; Martin A. Sullivan, "U.S. Multinationals Shifting Profits Out of the United States," Tax Notes, March 10, 2008, p. 1078-1082; and Martin A. Sullivan, "Shifting of Profits Offshore Costs U.S. Treasury $10 Billion or More," Tax Notes, September 27, 2004, p. 1477-1481.

Figure 4. Corporate Tax Revenue as a Percentage of GDP, 1946-2010

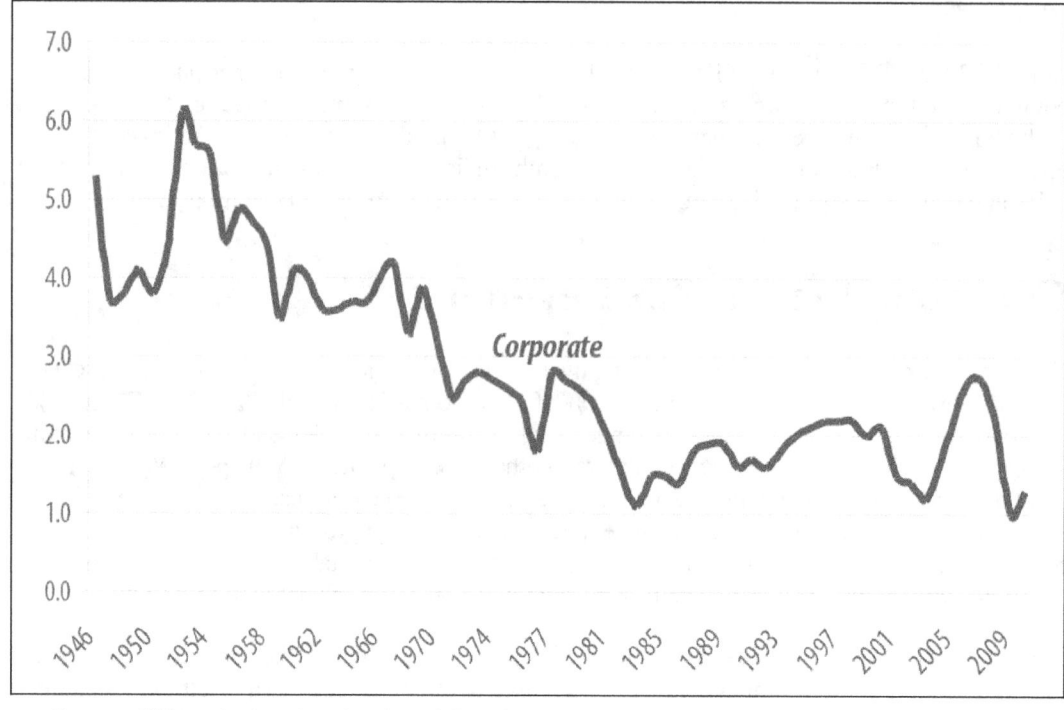

Source: CRS graphic based on data from Office of Management and Budget, Table 2.3, http://www.whitehouse.gov/omb/budget/Historicals.

International Comparisons

Tax Rates

Comparisons between corporate tax rates in the United States and those found elsewhere in the world are made frequently. The focus among non-economists tends to be on comparing statutory rates. Economists, however, generally prefer to compare effective tax rates when making international comparisons. The reason for this is that every country has a different tax system, and the statutory tax rate is just one component of each system. For example, some countries may have higher or lower rates, allow for faster capital recovery (i.e., deprecation), or offer corporate tax credits not offered by other countries. Effective tax rates attempt to account for all the system differences and are more indicative of the tax burden in each country.

When making comparisons between U.S. and worldwide tax rates it is also important to indicate whether tax rates are simple (unweighted) averages or whether they are adjusted (weighted) to account for the size of the economies being compared. If the U.S. tax rate is compared to world tax rates that do not account for the size of other economies, then a small economy, such as Iceland, can have the same effect on the average international rate as a large economy, such as Germany or Japan. It is therefore more appropriate to compare the U.S. tax rate to a weighted average of international tax rates. Typically, each country's tax rate is weighted by its gross domestic product (GDP) when computing the average.

Table 2 compares the statutory tax rate, the weighted effective rate, and the weighted effective marginal rate in the United States to the rest of the Organization for Economic Co-operation and Development (OECD) countries. While the U.S. statutory tax rate is about 10 percentage points higher than the other OECD countries, the U.S. effective tax rate is about the same as effective rates found elsewhere. The OECD, however, excludes several large economies, in particular China and Brazil.[36] **Table 2** also shows that the tax rate most relevant for investment decisions—the weighted effective marginal rate—is also similar between the United States and the rest of the world.

Table 2. Corporate Tax Rates: Comparing the United States to the Rest of the OECD

Tax Rate Measure	United States	OECD
Statutory	39.2%	29.6%
Weighted Effective Tax Rate	27.1%	27.7%
Weighted Effective Marginal Tax Rate	20.2%	18.3%

Source: CRS Report R41743, *International Corporate Tax Rate Comparisons and Policy Implications*, by Jane G. Gravelle.

Notes: The statutory and weighted effective tax rate come from Table 1 in the cited CRS report. The weighted effective marginal rate comes from Table 6. See the discussion in the cited report for more information about the methodology used for the tax rate estimates.

Tax Revenues

Corporate tax revenues in U.S. are below the average of all OECD member countries. **Figure 5** displays corporate tax revenues for OECD member countries as a percentage of GDP for 2009. The average OECD member collected corporate taxes equal to 2.8% of GDP compared to the U.S. which collected revenues equal to about 1.9% of GDP. Corporate tax receipts in the United States have been below the OECD average since 1997, and before that they fluctuated closely around the OECD average. Aside from a few outliers, most OECD countries collect revenue within a couple percentage points of each other.

There are a couple of reasons why the United States collects less in federal corporate tax revenue than other countries. For example, as **Figure 4** shows, corporate tax revenues in the United States have generally declined since WWII. At the same time, corporate tax revenues in other OECD countries (particularly European countries), have remained relatively stable even in the face of declining tax rates.[37] Some countries have adopted base broadening policies to offset tax rate decreases, typically in the form of reduced investment credits, less generous loss offset rules, and limitations on interest deductibility and depreciation.[38] Recent research also suggests that there has been a shift from the non-corporate to corporate sector in some countries, and that in other

---

[36] OECD members are generally countries with advanced economies. The OECD works closely with other large economies that are less economically advanced. For more information on current OECD members, see http://www.oecd.org/about/membersandpartners/.

[37] Ruud A. DeMooij and Gaetan Nicodeme, *Corporate Tax Policy, Entrepreneurship and Incorporation in the EU*, European Commission, Directorate-General for Economic and Financial Affairs, No. 263, January 2007, p.6. http://ec.europa.eu/economy_finance/publications/publication808_en.pdf.

[38] *Ibid.*, p. 13.

countries limited liability outside the corporate form is not available, making it more attractive to shift to a corporate form.[39] Combined, these factors appear to explain why corporate tax rates have fallen elsewhere while revenues have held steady.

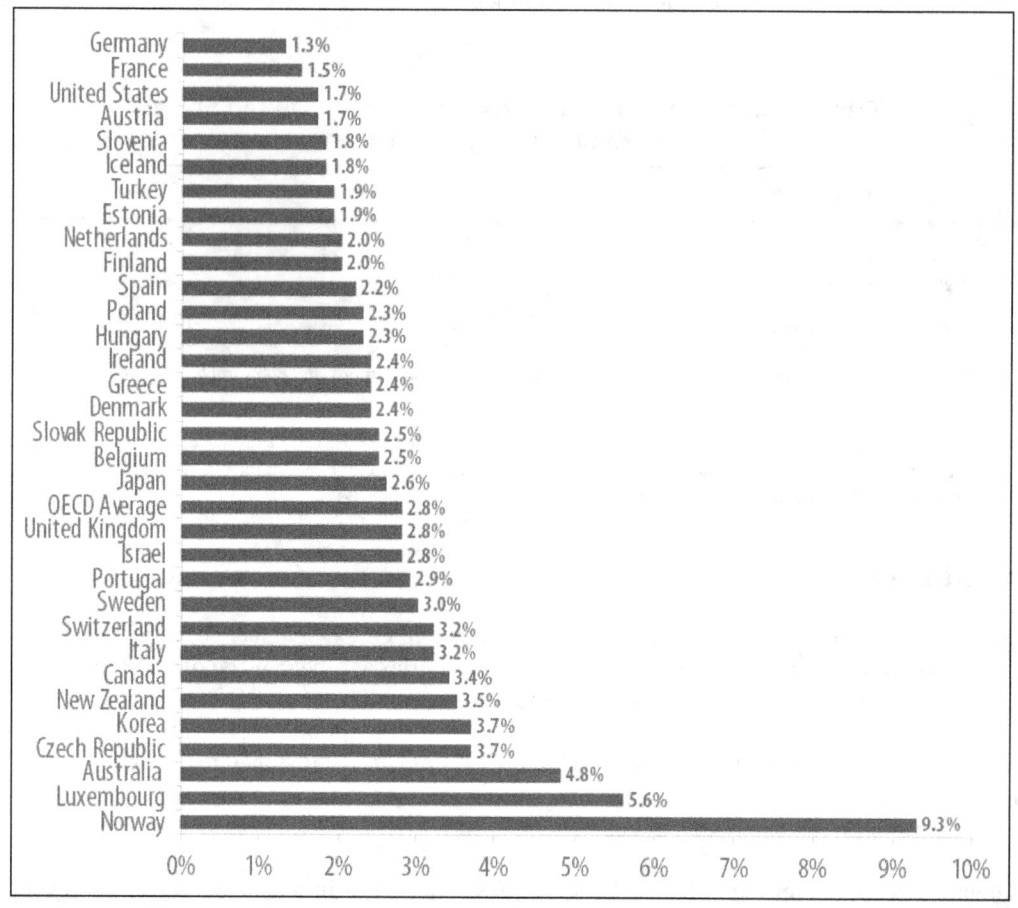

Figure 5. Corporate Tax Revenue as a Percentage of GDP in 2009
OECD Member Countries

Source: CRS graphic based on data from OECD, Revenue Statistics, Comparative Tables, http://stats.oecd.org/Index.aspx?DataSetCode=REV.

Notes: Chili and Mexico had missing data and were therefore excluded from this analysis.

---

[39] U.S. Department of the Treasury, *Treasury Conference on Business Taxation and Global Competitiveness: Background Paper*, July 23, 2007, p. 18, http://www.treasury.gov/press-center/press-releases/Documents/07230%20r.pdf.

Economic Considerations

Why Have a Corporate Income Tax?

A variety of reasons have been offered to justify the corporate tax since the enactment of the Corporate Tax Act of 1909 (P.L. 61-4). To avoid constitutionality issues, Congress structured the tax as an excise tax on the privilege of doing business in the corporate form (i.e., limited liability and access to capital markets).[40] While the new corporate income tax was challenged by several corporations that claimed it to be unconstitutional, the Supreme Court accepted its rationale and ruled that the privilege of doing business in the corporate form could be measured by profits.[41] The privileged-based rationale for the corporate tax is generally not accepted by economists today. Economists tend to view the risk-sharing from limited liability and pooling of resources as beneficial to the economy.

The corporate tax system serves to ensure a comprehensive income tax system. Absent a corporate income tax, corporate earnings would not be taxed until they were paid out to individuals. Thus, corporations would have an incentive to avoid taxes by retaining earnings.[42] Shareholders would avoid taxes so long as corporations did not pay out earnings. Further, shareholders would benefit when corporations retained earnings over long periods of time, as delaying payouts would reduce the present value of the tax burden (assuming no change in tax rates over time).[43]

Some economists also favor the corporate tax as a tax on profits, or economic rents.[44] Economic rents are profit levels above the required rate of return for factors of production (e.g., labor, capital). If the corporate tax could be designed to tax only pure profits or economic rents,[45] the corporate tax would not induce efficiency losses. Firms maximize profits by optimizing on output and price. Taxes on pure profits or economic rents do not distort a firm's choice of output, and thus do induce distortions or efficiency losses. In practice, since pure profits and economic rents are difficult to measure, taxes are levied on accounting profits as described above (see "Structure of the Corporate Income Tax"). Thus, the corporate tax as currently applied is not a tax on pure profits or economic rents. Consequently, the corporate tax in its current form does distort economic decision making, which can reduce overall economic output.

---

[40] In 1895, the Supreme Court found that an income tax enacted a year earlier was unconstitutional because it was a direct tax not apportioned among the states according to population. See *Pollock v. Farmers' Loan and Trust Co*, 157 U.S. 429 (1895). The individual income tax was enacted in 1913, following ratification of the sixteenth amendment (Amendment XVI) to the United States Constitution, which allowed Congress to levy an income tax without apportioning in among the states.

[41] Joseph A. Pechman, *Federal Tax Policy*, 4 ed. (Washington, DC: The Brookings Institute, 1983), p. 129.

[42] Organisation for Economic Co-Operation and Development (OECD), *Reforming Corporate Income Tax*, Policy Brief, July 2008, http://www.oecd.org/tax/taxpolicyanalysis/41069272.pdf.

[43] Additionally, a significant share of gain is never taxed given the current structure of the estate tax system. Heirs, as recipients of corporate stock, are not taxed on the decedent's gain.

[44] Organisation for Economic Co-Operation and Development (OECD), *Reforming Corporate Income Tax*, Policy Brief, July 2008, http://www.oecd.org/tax/taxpolicyanalysis/41069272.pdf.

[45] A pure tax on profits would tax only economic profits, where economic profits are revenues less both accounting costs and economic costs, such as the opportunity costs associated with a firms' factors of production. The opportunity cost of labor, for example, is the wage that would be earned by labor if that labor were employed by or engaged in the most attractive alternative activity.

An alternative to having a corporate tax would be to directly tax the factors of production that make up the corporation (i.e., labor and capital). This option would eliminate the corporate tax entirely, effectively taxing all corporations as pass-through entities. While this approach represents one way to address concerns of double taxation on corporate profits, it would leave open the possibility that corporations could be used to shelter income if unrealized capital gains remained untaxed.[46]

Corporate Tax Incidence

Since corporations are legal, not physical entities, corporations cannot actually bear the burden of taxes. Instead, the tax is passed along to individuals connected with corporations, including corporate owners (shareholders), workers, and customers. For example, the tax could be passed along to these individuals in the form of lower dividends or capital gains (corporate owners), reduced salaries and fringe benefits (employees), or higher prices (customers).

Traditional analysis of the corporate tax, in a closed economy, indicates that it is corporate owners who bear the tax burden, and the owners of capital more generally in the long-run.[47] In contrast, a number of more recent theoretical studies find that labor can bear the majority of the tax burden, in an open economy.[48] The theoretical findings, however, appear to rely critically on particular assumptions that drive the results. When these assumptions are relaxed the burden of the corporate tax is found to fall mostly on capital—in line with the traditional analysis.

In recent years, a number of economists have taken a statistical (empirical) approach to determine the incidence of the corporate tax. While these studies tend to conclude that a substantial portion of the corporate tax burden falls on labor, methodological limitations lead these results to be questioned.[49] Given the unreliability of recent empirical research, and the consistency of traditional theoretical models, some economists have been reluctant to move away from traditional incidence assumptions, where owners of capital are assumed to bear most of the burden of the corporate tax.

Government agencies that analyze how the incidence of the corporate tax is distributed have recently changed incidence assumptions used in producing distribution tables.[50] The Congressional Budget Office (CBO) now assumes that 75% of the burden of the corporate income tax falls to owners of capital, with the remaining 25% assigned to households in proportion to their labor income.[51] Prior to this change, the entire burden of the corporate tax was

---

[46] For further discussion, see "Integration of the Corporate and Individual Tax Systems" in the "Options for Reform" section below.

[47] The traditional view on the incidence of the corporate tax originated with the development of the "Harberger model" in 1962 and subsequent refinements. See Arnold Harberger, "The Incidence of the Corporate Tax," The Journal of Political Economy, vol. 70 (June 1962), pp. 215-240.

[48] A review and critique of recent theoretical research, as well as a discussion of the extensions of the Harberger model can be found in Jennifer C. Gravelle, "Corporate Tax Incidence: Review of General Equilibrium Estimates and Analysis" Congressional Budget Office, Working Paper 2010-03, May 2010.

[49] These studies are reviewed in Jennifer C. Gravelle, *Corporate Tax Incidence: A Review of Empirical Estimates and Analysis*, Congressional Budget Office, Working Paper 2011-1, Washington, DC, June 2011 and CRS Report RL34229, *Corporate Tax Reform: Issues for Congress*, by Jane G. Gravelle and Thomas L. Hungerford.

[50] The Joint Committee on Taxation (JCT) does not assign corporate tax incidence to individuals.

[51] CBO provides background information on the changes in corporate tax rate distribution assumptions in Congressional Budget Office, *The Distribution of Household Income and Federal Taxes, 2008 and 2009*, Washington, (continued...)

assumed to be borne by owners of capital. Until 2008, the Department of the Treasury made a similar assumption. Recently, however, the Treasury changed their incidence assumption, such that 82% of the corporate income tax burden is allocated to owners of capital, and 18% to labor income.[52]

The recent change in corporate tax incidence assumptions has important implications for policy analysis. When it is assumed that the entire burden of the corporate tax is borne by capital, revenue-neutral changes in the tax burden do not change the distribution of the tax burden. This means that base-broadening, rate reducing tax reforms would not change how the tax burden is allocated across households. For example, a corporate tax rate cut financed by decreased depreciation deductions would not change the distribution of the corporate tax. However, under the new methodology, where a portion of the corporate tax burden falls on labor, changes in tax rates and changes in deductions that are revenue-neutral may change how the tax burden is distributed. Rate cuts financed by reduced depreciation deduction allowances, for example, would tend to reduce the progressivity of the corporate tax system when part of the burden falls on labor, as assumed by the Treasury.[53]

Evaluating the Corporate Income Tax

Several metrics can be used to evaluate the corporate tax system. These metrics can also help policymakers evaluate proposed reforms to the current system. One metric, equity, evaluates how the corporate tax burden is distributed across individuals. Generally, it is believed that the corporate income tax contributes to the overall progressivity of the U.S. tax system.[54] A second metric, efficiency, looks at potential distortions in economic activity that result from the corporate tax system or specific provisions within that system. The third metric discussed here is "competitiveness." Policymakers frequently note that the U.S. tax system should be competitive. This precise definition of this concept, however, is often unclear. Finally, an ideal tax system would be simple, such that both the costs imposed on taxpayers of complying with the tax system and administrative costs are minimized.

Equity

Some economists believe that the corporate income tax contributes to the overall progressivity of the tax system. CBO periodically publishes statistics on the distribution of federal taxes and

---

(...continued)
DC, July 2012, pp. 13-15, http://www.cbo.gov/sites/default/files/cbofiles/attachments/43373-AverageTaxRates_screen.pdf.

[52] Julie-Anne Cronin, Emily Y. Lin, and Laura Power, et al., *Distributing the Corporate Income Tax: Revised U.S. Treasury Methodology*, Office of Tax Analysis, Department of the Treasury, Technical Paper 5, Washington, DC, May 2012. Part of the tax on capital is allocated to owners of capital in general, with another portion allocated to capital earning economic rents.

[53] This result arises in part since rate changes are predicted to affect normal returns to capital, labor, and supernormal returns to capital. Changes in depreciation deductions are predicted to affect normal returns to capital and labor. Because higher income persons receive a disproportionate share of the supernormal returns to capital, rate cuts provide a greater benefit to higher income groups.

[54] Tax system progressivity is measured by the proportion of taxes paid by various income groups, relative to their share of income received.

household income.[55] Corporate income taxes are estimated to be highly progressive. The average corporate income tax rate paid by those in the top 1% of the income distribution is 5.2% (see **Table 3**). Those in the bottom quintile of the income distribution have an average tax rate of 0.5%. Further, in 2009, households in the top earnings quintile paid 77.2% of all corporate taxes (while earning 50.0% of pretax income). CBO estimates that households in the bottom quintile paid less than 2% of all corporate tax liabilities, while earning 7.7% of all pretax income.

In allocating the burden of the corporate income tax across households, CBO assumed that 75% of the burden was borne by owners of capital, while the remaining 25% was allocated to labor income. Previous CBO studies evaluating the distribution of federal taxes allocated the entire economic burden of the corporate income tax to owners of capital.[56]

Table 3. CBO's Distribution of Corporate Income Tax
2009

Before-tax Income Group	Average Corporate Income Tax Rate (%)	Share of Corporate Income Tax Liabilities (%)	Share of Pretax Income (%)
Lowest Quintile	0.5	1.8	7.7
Second Quintile	0.5	3.2	9.7
Middle Quintile	0.6	5.8	13.8
Fourth Quintile	0.7	10.2	20.1
Highest Quintile	2.3	77.2	50.0
All Households	1.5	100.0	100.0
91st to 95th Percentiles	1.1	7.4	9.9
96th to 99th Percentiles	1.7	14.1	12.4
Top 1%	5.2	47.1	13.3

Source: Congressional Budget Office.

Notes: The CBO assumes that 25% of the corporate income tax is allocated to workers in proportion to their labor income. Changing the portion of the corporate tax burden allocated to labor would change the estimated distribution of the corporate tax burden (see the section "Corporate Tax Incidence" below).

The Treasury recently has started distributing a portion of the corporate tax burden (18%) to labor income.[57] The implications of this assumption are illustrated in **Table 4**. Treasury estimates suggest that, in 2012, if the entire burden of the corporate income tax were allocated to capital, taxpayers in the highest quintile would bear 80.9%. If it is assumed that 18% of the corporate tax burden falls on labor income (as is assumed by the Treasury), that share falls to 76.0%. Alternatively, if half of the corporate tax income were assumed to be borne by labor income

---

[55] Congressional Budget Office, *Average Federal Tax Rates in 2007*, Washington, DC, June 2010, http://www.cbo.gov/sites/default/files/cbofiles/attachments/AverageFedTaxRates2007.pdf.

[56] For further discussion of the distribution of corporate tax burdens, see "Corporate Tax Incidence" above.

[57] See the section "Corporate Tax Incidence" above.

earners, the share of the corporate tax burden falling on the top income quintile would be 68.9%. Generally, the larger the share of the corporate tax burden that is assumed to fall on labor, the less progressive the corporate tax appears.

Table 4. Treasury's Distribution of Corporate Income Tax
2012

Cash Income Group	82% Capital / 18% Labor	100% Capital	50% Capital / 50% Labor
Lowest Quintile	1.1	0.8	1.4
Second Quintile	3.2	2.3	4.6
Middle Quintile	6.6	5.2	8.8
Fourth Quintile	12.0	9.7	15.8
Highest Quintile	76.0	80.9	68.9
All Households	100.0	100.0	100.0
Top 10%	66.1	72.8	56.0
Top 1%	43.0	49.8	30.6

Source: Julie-Anne Cronin, Emily Y. Lin, and Laura Power, et al., *Distributing the Corporate Income Tax: Revised U.S. Treasury Methodology*, Office of Tax Analysis, Department of the Treasury, Technical Paper 5, Washington, DC, May 2012.

Efficiency

Economic inefficiencies arise when taxes distort market choices. When businesses and individuals make choices that are motivated by taxes, economic resources may not be put to their most productive use. Corporate tax reforms and corporate tax systems designed to minimize economic distortions can help promote an efficient economy. Generally, tax systems that impose large tax rates on broad tax bases limit tax-induced distortions in economic activity.

Broadly, the corporate tax system distorts the allocation of capital across economic sectors. The corporate tax may reduce economic efficiency to the extent that it causes a misallocation of capital between corporate and noncorporate business forms.[58] Certain provisions in the tax code, which lead to different effective tax rates on different types of investments, can also distort the allocation of resources (see the effective tax rate discussion in the section "Which Companies Pay?" above).

Some of the exemptions, credits, deductions, and other tax preferences in the U.S. tax system represent attempts to address instances where markets fail to maximize economic efficiency. Take, for example, tax incentives for research and development (R&D) related activities.[59] R&D

---

[58] Further discussion can be found in CRS Report RL34229, *Corporate Tax Reform: Issues for Congress*, by Jane G. Gravelle and Thomas L. Hungerford.

[59] For background on tax incentives for R&D, see CRS Report RL31181, *Research Tax Credit: Current Law, Legislation in the 112th Congress, and Policy Issues*, by Gary Guenther.

that leads to technological innovation is associated with positive externalities. That is, there are benefits to R&D that accrue to those not directly involved in or paying for the research itself. Economic theory suggests that activities that generate positive externalities tend to be underprovided by markets. Thus, providing a tax subsidy for R&D, thereby directing additional economic resources to R&D related activities, could lead to additional R&D and improve overall economic efficiency.[60]

Tax preferences that narrow the tax base may necessitate higher tax rates to raise sufficient federal revenues over time. The potential for economic distortions caused by higher marginal rates should be weighed against the potential efficiency gains associated with various tax preferences. Tax preferences or tax expenditures that narrow the tax base, that do not otherwise enhance economic efficiency, can ultimately reduce economic efficiency by requiring higher marginal rates over time.[61] Features of the U.S. corporate tax system that contribute to varying tax burdens across different asset types include the design of accelerated depreciation rules and the Section 199 production activities deduction.[62]

Removing certain provisions, such as accelerated depreciation, in exchange for reduced tax rates, will not necessarily improve economic efficiency. Slowing depreciation, and making depreciation more neutral across different types of assets, could increase the cost of capital. Modifying depreciation to be more neutral across assets while reducing the corporate tax rate provides a windfall benefit to existing capital. The burden on new investments increases, but all capital benefits from reduced tax rates.[63]

The U.S. corporate tax system also contains a tax-induced bias towards debt financing, which raises economic efficiency concerns. The primary factor contributing to this bias is the fact that interest payments can be deducted from income, while dividend payments can not.[64] Rising levels of corporate debt, and the possible contribution of high debt levels to the recent global economic crisis, have increased policymakers' interest in evaluating the current tax treatment of debt.[65] Empirical evidence does suggest that tax policy affects firms' debt choices. For example, a recent study summarizing the results of the literature found that a one percentage point increase in tax

---

[60] The effectiveness of the research tax credit depends on whether the credit motivates additional research activity, rather than simply reward companies for engaging in research activity that would have taken place without a tax credit. For more on this issue, see U.S. Government Accountability Office, *The Research Tax Credit's Design and Administration Can Be Improved*, GAO-10-136, November 2009, http://www.gao.gov/new.items/d10136.pdf.

[61] The government also has alternative revenue generating options, including taxes on individuals. If less revenue is raised through the corporate tax system, the federal government may look to alternative revenue sources.

[62] Table 8 in CRS Report RL34229, *Corporate Tax Reform: Issues for Congress*, by Jane G. Gravelle and Thomas L. Hungerford illustrates the effect of depreciation rates and the Section 199 deduction on the tax burden of different assets. See also Testimony of Jane G. Gravelle, Senate Committee on Finance, *Tax Reform Options: Incentives for Capital Investment and Manufacturing*, March 6, 2012, http://www.finance.senate.gov/imo/media/doc/Testimony%20of%20Jane%20Gravelle.pdf.

[63] For further explanation and numerical examples, see See also Testimony of Jane G. Gravelle, Senate Committee on Finance, *Tax Reform Options: Incentives for Capital Investment and Manufacturing*, March 6, 2012, http://www.finance.senate.gov/imo/media/doc/Testimony%20of%20Jane%20Gravelle.pdf.

[64] Reduced tax rates on dividends and capital gains help reduce the debt-equity bias by reducing double-taxation for equity investments.

[65] In July 2011, the Committee on Ways and Means and Senate Finance Committee held a joint hearing titled *Tax Reform and the Tax Treatment of Debt and Equity*. Witness testimony is available at http://waysandmeans.house.gov/Calendar/EventSingle.aspx?EventID=250212.

rates increased the debt-asset ratio between 0.17 and 0.28.[66] Overall, the size of the distortion has been estimated to be less than 5% of corporate tax revenues.[67]

The differential treatment of domestic and foreign-source income by U.S. multinationals also raises concerns that business decisions of U.S. multinational corporations may be motivated by tax policy. If multinational corporations allocate resources differently than they would under a neutral tax policy, current tax policy creates economic inefficiencies.[68] If, however, resource reallocation in response to tax rate differentials is limited (i.e., there is limited capital mobility), then efficiency losses may be small.[69]

Finally, the economic efficiency of the corporate tax depends on what is actually being taxed. If a corporate tax can be designed such that the tax is levied on only economic profits,[70] the tax should not change firms' output decisions in the short-run, and thus should have limited efficiency consequences.[71] In practice, however, the corporate tax is not levied on pure economic profits. The opportunity cost of capital is included in the tax base. In this sense, the corporate tax acts as a tax on capital, and could discourages capital formation in the corporate sector.

Competitiveness

Policymakers often use "competitiveness" as a rationale for corporate tax reform.[72] Economists, however, question whether "competitiveness" makes sense as a tax policy objective for a country. For economists, the typical objective is economic efficiency, or the optimal use of limited resources.

---

[66] See Ruud de Mooij, *The Tax Elasticity of Corporate Debt: A Synthesis of Size and Variations*, International Monetary Fund, Working Paper, WP-11-95, April, 2011, http://www.imf.org/external/pubs/ft/wp/2011/wp1195.pdf.

[67] The distortion appears small due to limited substitution between debt and equity. For more, see CRS Report RL34229, *Corporate Tax Reform: Issues for Congress*, by Jane G. Gravelle and Thomas L. Hungerford.

[68] For a discussion of efficiency considerations related to U.S. international tax policy, see U.S. Congress, Joint Committee on Taxation, *Economic Efficiency and Structural Analysis of Alternative U.S. Tax Policies for Foreign Direct Investment*, prepared by Joint Committee on Taxation, 110th Cong., June 25, 2008, JCX-55-08.

[69] See CRS Report RL34229, *Corporate Tax Reform: Issues for Congress*, by Jane G. Gravelle and Thomas L. Hungerford.

[70] Economic profits are profits that remain after all costs, including the opportunity costs of inputs, have been subtracted. While the U.S. tax system does allow for deductions for the cost of inputs, there are no deductions for the opportunity costs associated with the use of resources.

[71] Economic profits are those above the normal rate of return required for businesses to operate. Economic theory suggests that firms maximize profits by producing at the point where marginal revenue is equal to marginal cost. Profits are determined by the difference between the price and the average cost, times the number of units sold. A tax that is levied on profits does not affect either the marginal cost of production nor the marginal revenue. Thus, firms should not change their production decisions as a result of tax policy changes, in the short-run.

[72] For example, the Obama Administration has claimed a commitment to tax reform that will support competitiveness of American businesses by "increasing incentives to invest and hire in the United States by lowering rates, cutting tax expenditures, and reducing complexity, while being fiscally responsible." See The White House and the Department of the Treasury, *The President's Framework for Business Tax Reform*, February 2012, p. 1, http://www.treasury.gov/resource-center/tax-policy/Documents/The-Presidents-Framework-for-Business-Tax-Reform-02-22-2012.pdf. Representative Dave Camp, Chairman of the Committee on Ways and Means, supports moving to a territorial-based tax system, claiming that such a policy "makes American companies more competitive on the global stage." Committee on Ways and Means, "Camp Releases International Tax Reform Discussion Draft," press release, October 26, 2011, http://waysandmeans.house.gov/News/DocumentSingle.aspx?DocumentID=266168.

From an economic perspective, growth is not a zero-sum game, or something for which countries compete. Enhanced economic well-being in one country generally does not reduce economic opportunities in other countries. In fact, if one country experiences economic growth, those benefits tend to spill over to that country's trading partners, as higher domestic incomes increase the demand for imported goods and services. Trade between nations can benefits all countries involved. Thus, while individual firms may compete, countries trade.[73]

Much of the confusion surrounding the concept of "competitiveness" as a tax policy objective stems from the fact that what it means for a country to be "competitive" is not clearly defined. Some economists, in an attempt to define "competitiveness," have noted that "competitive" policies are those that promote domestic business globally, while increasing the U.S. standards of living.[74] Krugman (1994) argues that this and similar definitions are flawed, noting that "the growth rate of living standards essentially equals the rate of domestic productivity growth—not productivity relative to competitors."[75] The direct policy objective of promoting domestic business globally is also not clear. Is the goal to have tax policies that encourage U.S. firms to invest abroad, to better compete in international markets? Or is the goal to prevent the movement of U.S. business operations overseas? These two are different policy objectives often promoted in the name of "competitiveness."[76] Given the confusion surrounding "competitiveness" as a policy objective, keeping the focus on the economic objectives of neutrality and economic efficiency could prove useful in designing tax policy that maximizes output and well-being.

Simplicity and Administrability

Complexity in the tax code contributes to increased compliance costs, as complex tax systems require taxpayers devote more time and economic resources to tax preparation.[77] Tax code compliance creates inefficiencies to the extent that resources devoted to tax preparation are not available for other productive activities. Further, complex tax systems may put certain taxpayers at a disadvantage, as those with limited resources may not be able to claim all tax benefits to which they are legally entitled.[78] Thus, complex tax systems may be viewed as unfair or

---

[73] Numerous economists have made this point, including Paul Krugman, "Competitiveness: A Dangerous Obsession," *Foreign Affairs*, vol. 73, no. 2 (March/April 1994), pp. 28-44 and Jane G. Gravelle, Does the Concept of Competitiveness Have Meaning in Formulating Corporate Tax Policy? November 2011, forthcoming, *Tax Law Review*, at http://www.americantaxpolicyinstitute.org/pdf/Jane%20Gravelle%20paper.pdf.

[74] See, for example, Richard H.K. Vietor and Matthew Weinzierl, "Macroeconomic Policy and U.S. Competitiveness," *Harvard Business Review*, March 2012, pp. http://hbr.org/2012/03/macroeconomic-policy-and-us-competitiveness/ar/1.

[75] Paul Krugman, "Competitiveness: A Dangerous Obsession," *Foreign Affairs*, vol. 73, no. 2 (March/April 1994), p. 34.

[76] For further discussion, see Jane G. Gravelle, Does the Concept of Competitiveness Have Meaning in Formulating Corporate Tax Policy? November 2011, forthcoming, *Tax Law Review*, at http://www.americantaxpolicyinstitute.org/pdf/Jane%20Gravelle%20paper.pdf.

[77] Estimates suggest that costs associated with tax compliance are roughly 1% of GDP. This estimate includes costs of complying with individual as well as corporate income taxes. See U.S. Government Accountability Office, *Summary of Estimates of the Costs of the Federal Tax System*, GAO-05-878, August 2005, http://www.gao.gov/new.items/d05878.pdf.

[78] It has been reported that small- and mid-sized companies forgo certain tax benefits because the costs associated with claiming tax benefits exceeds the value of certain incentives. See John D. McKinnon, "Firms Pass Up Tax Breaks, Citing Hassles, Complexity," *Wall Street Journal*, July 23, 2012, p. A1, U.S. Edition.

inequitable. Tax code complexity also increases administrative and enforcement costs. Simplifying the current tax system could help reduce the tax gap.[79]

Options for Reform

Broader Base, Lower Rates

Corporate tax reform discussions have generally focused on reducing the top corporate tax rate and offsetting the revenue loss by increasing the amount of income subject to tax (i.e., broadening the tax base). If revenue neutrality is a goal then a reduction in the corporate tax rate is limited by how much the tax base can be expanded. The rate can be reduced further (to zero) or the base made less broad if revenue loss is not a concern. Revenue loss may not be an option given the government's current and future revenue needs. Some have suggested that cutting the corporate tax rate below its current top rate of 35% could increase revenue. A recent CRS report reviewed and critiqued the literature that purportedly supports this argument and found that the claims that behavioral responses could cause revenues to rise if rates were cut does not hold up on either a theoretical or an empirical basis.[80]

How much could the corporate tax rate be reduced while achieving revenue neutrality? The Joint Committee on Taxation (JCT) has estimated that relying solely on elimination of corporate tax expenditures, the rate could be reduced to 28%, although this proposal did not include the repeal of deferral.[81] The JCT estimates are only revenue neutral through a 10-year budget window. Some provisions, such as treatment of depreciation, change the timing of revenue, but not the total amount. Thus, estimates that are revenue-neutral through the 10-year budget window may not be revenue neutral over other time frames. It is estimated that a long-run revenue neutral corporate tax rate of 29.4% is attainable when the JCT estimates are adjusted to account for this timing effect and deferral is included.[82]

The top corporate rate could be reduced further if other changes were made in addition to eliminating all corporate tax expenditures. For example, the deductibility of interest, which is not a tax expenditure, could be restricted or eliminated. Additional revenues could be raised through the individual income tax system to pay for a corporate rate reduction. Examples of such options include, higher capital gains tax rates, accrual taxation of gains on corporate stock, and limits or modest taxes on retirement savings (which would benefit from corporate rate reductions), changes to tax preferences available to noncorporate businesses, and other reforms to business taxation.[83] At the same time, if the corporate tax rate is reduced, and tax reforms to the

---

[79] The Internal Revenue Service (IRS) defines the *gross* tax gap as the difference between the aggregate tax liability imposed by law for a given tax year and the amount of tax that taxpayers pay *voluntarily* and timely for that year. Relative to the size of corporate tax revenues, the tax gap is generally believed to be small. For additional background, see CRS Report R41582, *Tax Gap, Tax Enforcement, and Tax Compliance Proposals in the 112th Congress*, by James M. Bickley.

[80] CRS Report RL34229, *Corporate Tax Reform: Issues for Congress*, by Jane G. Gravelle and Thomas L. Hungerford.

[81] Memo from Thomas A. Barthold, Joint Committee on Taxation, October 27, 2011.

[82] See CRS Report RL34229, *Corporate Tax Reform: Issues for Congress*, by Jane G. Gravelle and Thomas L. Hungerford.

[83] See CRS Report R41743, *International Corporate Tax Rate Comparisons and Policy Implications*, by Jane G. Gravelle.

noncorporate sector are enacted, some business activity may return to the corporate sector, naturally broadening the base. Other business tax reforms may include changes to the taxation of American multinationals operating overseas. If these reforms reduced profit shifting to low-tax countries, the domestic corporate tax base may expand.[84]

It is important to think about how to broaden the corporate tax base.[85] Most of the largest corporate tax expenditures have an effect on marginal investment decisions. For example, expensing of research and experimental expenditures, accelerated depreciation, and the low-income housing tax credit, all increase the after-tax returns to investment. The Section 199 production activities deduction reduces marginal tax rates. Removing these types of expenditures could increase the effective tax rate on capital investment, which would likely reduce investment, and therefore output and short-run employment. There are a limited number of corporate tax expenditures that could be repealed without increasing marginal tax rates on investment. Thus, designing a revenue-neutral base-broadening corporate tax reform that does not increase marginal tax rates on investment leaves limited room for rate reduction.[86]

Revenue-neutral tax reform that eliminated corporate tax expenditures in exchange for a reduced corporate tax rate will likely increase the tax burden on some industries, while decreasing the burden on others. Sectors that rely heavily on the research credit, such as the computers and electronics industry, could see their tax burden increase if the research credit were repealed to pay for a corporate rate reduction. Sullivan (2011) analyzes a hypothetical revenue-neutral corporate tax reform that slows depreciation, repeals the Section 199 deduction, and repeals the research credit, in exchange for a corporate rate reduction to 30%.[87] Industries that would see the largest decline in their effective tax rates in Sullivan's analysis include securities, insurance, credit intermediation, and retail trade. Industries that would see that largest increase in effective tax rates include the computers and electronics, transport equipment, and electrical products sectors. Generally, Sullivan's hypothetical revenue-neutral corporate tax reform would increase effective tax rates on the manufacturing sector.

Corporate tax base broadening, depending on its design, could have unintended consequences for pass-through businesses. Pass-throughs would generally not benefit from a reduction in corporate tax rates, since their income is not subject to the corporate tax. Additionally, since not all "corporate" tax benefits are exclusively available to corporations, depending on how corporate tax benefits are scaled back to offset a rate reduction, pass-throughs could see their tax burden increase. Generally, business-related tax incentives are available to businesses that pay taxes through the individual and corporate income tax system.[88]

---

[84] Conversely, if corporate tax reforms increase the incentive to shift profits overseas, the domestic corporate tax base could shrink.

[85] For an analysis of how the way the base is broadened could effect the economy, see Nicholas Bull, Tim Dowd, and Pamela Moomau, "Corporate Tax Reform: A Macroeconomic Perspective," *National Tax Journal*, vol. 64, no. 4 (2011), pp. 923-942.

[86] Similarly, some base-broadening measures could harm, rather than promote, economic efficiency. For more on this issue see Alan D. Viard, "Two Cheers for Corporate Tax Base Broadening," *National Tax Journal*, vol. 62, no. 3 (September 2009), pp. 399-412.

[87] For an analysis of how a revenue-neutral tax reform that slows depreciation and repeals the Section 199 deduction and research credits to pay for a corporate rate reduction would affect different industries, see Martin A. Sullivan, "Winners and Losers in Corporate Tax Reform," *Tax Notes*, February 14, 2011, pp. 731-734.

[88] For example, roughly 25% of the revenue cost of the Section 199 domestic production activities deduction is due to claims by the non-corporate sector. See CRS Report R41988, *The Section 199 Production Activities Deduction:* (continued...)

Integration of the Corporate and Individual Tax Systems

Subjecting corporate income to two levels of taxation introduces a number of economic distortions. The current tax treatment of corporate income leads to otherwise similar corporate and non-corporate business being taxed differently; it creates incentives for corporations to retain earnings rather than distribute them; and the ability of corporations to deduct interest but not dividends leads to a preferences for debt over equity financing.

The distortions created by the corporate tax could be reduced by combining, or integrating, the corporate and individual tax systems. There are a number of ways and degrees to which integration could be pursued, and the list of options presented here is not exhaustive. Any reform that involved even partial integration of the corporate and individual tax systems would require careful consideration of numerous administrative details. Because of this, the discussion that follows focuses on general integration options. A much more detailed and technical analysis of various integration options may be found in a 1992 Treasury report on the subject.[89] Another consideration is the potential revenue implications of an integration-based reform. Generally, integration of the corporate and individual tax systems would be expected to reduce federal revenues. If a goal of tax reform is revenue neutrality, additional revenue-raising options would need to be considered.

One integration approach would be to eliminate the corporate tax and allocate earnings directly to shareholders in a manner similar to which partnerships and S corporations allocate income to their partners and shareholders. In effect, C corporations, partnerships, and S corporations would be treated identically for tax-purposes, with all being treated as pass-throughs. The types of administrative issues that this approach raises include what corporate tax items are to be passed-through to shareholders; how will record keeping be handled (millions of shares are traded daily); what anti-abuse measures are needed to prevent the use of corporations as tax shelters? Inability to address these administrative challenges would likely make integration infeasible.

An approach related to shareholder allocation is one that would keep the corporate tax in place, but give shareholders a credit for corporate taxes paid. The corporate tax in this case would act as a withholding tax, which would likely address some of the tax sheltering concerns that arise with direct allocations to shareholders. Additionally, keeping the corporate tax in place may ease certain administrative burdens should policymakers decide some tax items should not pass-through to shareholders. Concerns surrounding the administrative complexity associated with a full integration approach of this type has led the Treasury's not recommending this approach in their 1992 report.[90]

(...continued)
Background and Analysis, by Molly F. Sherlock.

[89] The Department of the Treasury, *Integration of the Individual and Corporate Tax Systems: Taxing Business Income Once*, Washington, DC, January 1992, http://www.treasury.gov/resource-center/tax-policy/Documents/integration.pdf. For a summary of the Treasury report, see R. Glenn Hubbard, "Corporate Tax Integration: A View from the Treasury Department," *Journal of Economic Perspectives*, vol. 7, no. 1 (Winter 1993), pp. 115-132.

[90] R. Glenn Hubbard, "Corporate Tax Integration: A View From the Treasury Department ," *The Journal of Economic Perspectives*, vol. 7, no. 1 (Winter 1993), pp. 115-132.

Other Options for Reducing "Double Taxation" of Corporate Income

Allowing corporations to claim a deduction for dividends paid could reduce the "double taxation" of corporate income. This approach, however, would not fully eliminate the double taxation of corporate profits. A dividend deduction does not affect the taxation of capital gains. A dividend deduction would also make it more attractive for firms to distribute rather than retain earnings, thus reversing the current incentives for distributing or retaining earnings.

Rather than providing a deduction at the corporate level, double taxation could be reduced by eliminating taxes for shareholders on dividends and capital gains, or just dividends. If dividends and capital gains were both excluded from income, the double taxation of corporate income would effectively be eliminated. Excluding just dividends would achieve partial relief. Eliminating taxation of corporate income at the individual level would reduce progressivity in the tax system, since dividend and capital gains income is disproportionately earned by higher-income households. Additionally, allowing firms a deduction for dividends paid or reducing individual-level taxes on capital gains and dividends would reduce federal tax revenues.

Taxation of Pass-Through Income

One goal of some corporate tax reform proposals, and integration specifically, is to reduce the discrepancy in the taxation of corporate and non-corporate businesses. An option that would be consistent with this goal would be to subject certain pass-throughs to the corporate tax. Several policymakers and the Obama Administration have expressed interest in taxing the largest pass-throughs as corporations.[91] This interest appears to be rooted in concern over the reduction in corporate tax revenues over time, partly attributable to the shift in business activity away from the corporate sector, and the perceived inequity and inefficiencies that exist because two otherwise identical business are taxed differently simply because of their legal structure. Taxing large pass-throughs as corporations would also allow for lower tax rates as it would broaden the corporate tax base. Lower tax rates combined with a reduction in business tax disparity could improve business tax equity and the allocation of resources relative to current policy.

Depending on how "large" pass-throughs were identified, a relatively small percentage of businesses currently structured as pass-throughs could be affected by the corporate tax under certain reforms.[92] An estimated 0.3% of S corporations could be taxed as corporations if a "large"

---

[91] In early 2011, Senate Finance Committee Chairman Max Baucus suggested the possibility of taxing pass-throughs earning above a certain income as corporations. See, Nicola M. White and Drew Pierson, "Baucus Says Congress Should Look at Taxing Passthroughs as Corporations," *Tax Notes Today*, May 5, 2011. In addition, nearly all major tax reform proposals released recently have called for some kind of base broadening which can be used to reduce tax rates with the aim of improving the business tax environment. The President's Economic Recovery and Advisory Board, for example, specifically calls for examining the distinction between corporate and non-corporate forms, along with general base broadening, lower tax rates, and reduced complexity. See, President's Economic Recovery and Advisory Board, *The Report on Tax Reform Options: Simplicity, Compliance, and Corporate Taxation*, Washington, DC, August 2010, http://www.whitehouse.gov/sites/default/files/microsites/PERAB_Tax_Reform_Report.pdf. For a summary of other recent tax reform proposals see, CRS Report R41591, *Tax Reform: An Overview of Proposals in the 112th Congress*, by James M. Bickley. On March 7, 2012, the House Committee on Ways and Means held a hearing on the issue of pass-throughs taxation in the context of tax reform. Testimony given at that hearing may be found at http://waysandmeans.house.gov/Calendar/EventSingle.aspx?EventID=282644.

[92] CRS Report R42451, *Taxing Large Pass-Throughs As Corporations: How Many Firms Would Be Affected?*, by Mark P. Keightley

pass-through is defined as one with receipts exceeding $50 million (0.2% for partnerships).[93] Reducing this threshold to $10 million, an estimated 1.6% of S corporations could be taxed as corporations (0.8% for partnerships).[94]

Although estimates suggest that only a small percentage of pass-throughs could be considered large for corporate tax purposes, those firms are responsible for a significant amount of economic activity—indicating that the proposed policy change could raise substantial revenue. For example, 30% of S corporation receipts are generated by the largest 0.3% of S corporations, and 41% of partnership receipts are generated by the largest 0.2% of partnerships.[95]

International Tax: Territorial vs. Worldwide Taxation

Tax reform has raised an important question for policymakers with regards to American multi-nationals: is the current U.S. tax system for taxing American businesses with overseas operations appropriate in a globalized business environment, or is reform needed?[96] While the current U.S. system is occasionally referred to as a worldwide tax system, in reality it is actually a hybrid, containing features of both worldwide and territorial tax systems. In fact, no country has a pure form of either tax system, although most developed countries have moved more in the direction of a territorial tax regime.

The traditional metric used to evaluate an international tax system is how it affects investment location decisions. Economic theory states that worldwide output would be maximized if investments were taxed the same regardless of where they were made. In such an environment, taxes have no impact on where firms choose to invest. Instead, investments would be made in whichever location offered the highest rate of return, which, in turn, would result in resources being allocated most efficiently and output being maximized. Equalization of tax treatment across locations is most closely associated with a worldwide tax system. The current system U.S. tax system could be moved more in that direction if deferral of foreign earned income were not allowed and if the foreign tax credit limit were increased. While there have been proposals to limit the ability to defer income, worldwide-related proposals tend to move in the opposite direction with respect to the foreign tax credit, generally to prevent income shifting and to preserve the tax base (see the section "Comparing Current Corporate and Business Tax Reform Proposals").

Alternatively, a reform could be adopted that includes a transition to a territorial type system. Under a pure territorial system, the United States would forgo all income earned outside its boarders. A territorial system is argued to help domestic corporations compete in foreign markets

---

[93] *Ibid.*

[94] Using an asset-based measure of size produces similar estimates. It is estimated that between 0.3% and 1.0% of pass-throughs could pay the corporate tax depending on whether a $100 million or $25 million asset threshold is used to define a "large" firm.

[95] The largest 0.2% of S corporations hold 43% of S corporation assets, while the largest 1.1% of partnerships hold 78% of partnership assets.

[96] For more information on reform of the international tax system, see CRS Report RL34115, *Reform of U.S. International Taxation: Alternatives*, by Jane G. Gravelle; CRS Report R42624, *Moving to a Territorial Income Tax: Options and Challenges*, by Jane G. Gravelle; CRS Report R40623, *Tax Havens: International Tax Avoidance and Evasion*, by Jane G. Gravelle; and CRS Report R41743, *International Corporate Tax Rate Comparisons and Policy Implications*, by Jane G. Gravelle.

since they would face the same (foreign) tax rates as their competitors. But as was discussed previously (see the section titled "Competitiveness") countries, do not "compete" in any economic sense, they trade, and it is trade that helps determine the economic well-being of a country. Additionally, a territorial tax system does not necessarily enhance economic efficiency.

At the same time, a territorial system may lead to more investment in low-tax countries. Proponents have argued that a territorial system would lead to an increase in corporate repatriations (transfers in foreign subsidiary profits to U.S. parent companies), which would promote domestic investment and employment. A popular technique that has been proposed to transition to a territorial system is by providing a dividend exemption. With a dividend exemption, corporations would be allowed to repatriate income from their foreign-located subsidiaries via a divided payment and exempt, for example, 95% of that payment from taxation. Research has questioned the effect of dividend repatriation exemptions on domestic investment and employment.[97]

Another option would take a hybrid approach, with the goal of minimizing incentives to shelter money in tax havens. The opportunity to keep money abroad for real business operations would remain. One proposal would impose a minimum tax on foreign-earned income earned in countries with low tax rates. The tax would be applied to deferred income earned in countries with a tax below a particular rate, for example, 20%. Income earned in countries with rates below 20%, thereafter, would be subject to a current U.S. tax of 20%. The income earned in countries with rates above this level would be exempt from U.S. taxation. Some have expressed concern that designing such a minimum tax may be too complex.[98] An alternative to this approach that creates a "cliff" effect by encouraging firms to move investment to countries with tax rates just above the minimum is to impose an overall minimum tax with a credit for taxes paid.

Comparing Current Corporate and Business Tax Reform Proposals

In recent years, economists, lawmakers, and others have offered a number of business and corporate tax reform proposals. **Table 5** summarizes key comprehensive reforms proposed by Members of Congress and the Obama Administration. Also included in **Table 5** are the business and corporate tax reforms from the 2010 Fiscal Commission report.[99]

In February 2012, the Obama Administration released "The President's Framework for Business Tax Reform." The Administration's proposal would eliminate a number of corporate tax expenditures, and provides options for other corporate reforms.[100] The Administration claims that eliminating tax expenditures, while adopting other base-broadening reforms, could result in a

---

[97] CRS Report R40178, *Tax Cuts on Repatriation Earnings as Economic Stimulus: An Economic Analysis*, by Donald J. Marples and Jane G. Gravelle.

[98] This concern has been expressed by Ed Kleinbard, Professor of Law, University of Southern California Gould School of Law. Reported in Julie Martin, "Minimum Tax on Multinationals Could Slow Profit Shifting," *Tax Notes*, March 19, 2012.

[99] For additional details on tax reform as outlined by the Fiscal Commission, see CRS Report R41641, *Reducing the Budget Deficit: Tax Policy Options*, by Molly F. Sherlock.

[100] Other reforms that could be considered under the Administration's proposal include adjusting depreciation schedules, reducing tax-induced preferences for debt financing, and treating large pass-through entities as corporations.

revenue-neutral reduction in the corporate tax rate to 28%. The Administration's proposal would also provide enhanced tax incentives for manufacturers, small businesses, research activities, and clean energy.

The Administration's proposal also seeks to make changes to the current international tax system. Specifically, subsidiaries of U.S. corporations operating abroad would be required to pay a minimum tax on foreign-source income.[101] The Administration's proposal would also deny certain deductions associated with moving business operations abroad, provide tax credits for expenses associated with moving business activities back to the United States, and strengthen international tax rules that may allow firms to shift profits overseas or reduce U.S. taxes by taking deductions associated with overseas investment.

In October 2011, Chairman of the House Committee on Ways and Means, Representative David Camp, released a discussion draft on a proposal that would change the U.S. tax treatment of foreign-source income.[102] While the discussion draft did include text that would reduce the corporate tax rate to 25% (supporting documentation indicated that this rate reduction would be paid for with unspecified base-broadening provisions),[103] the focus of the discussion draft was on provisions that would shift the United States to a territorial tax system.

To shift towards a territorial tax, Chairman Camp's proposal would exempt 95% of certain foreign-source income from U.S. tax—including U.S. dividends paid to corporate shareholders owning at least 10% of shares.[104] Thus, generally, income earned abroad would not be subject to U.S. tax. The proposal also suggests options for certain provisions designed to prevent erosion of the corporate tax base, including use of Subpart F rules for certain passive and highly mobile income and thin capitalization rules to prevent interest deductions for borrowing in the United States that would finance overseas operations.

The Bipartisan Tax Fairness and Simplification Act of 2011 (S. 727), often referred to as the "Wyden-Coats proposal," proposes substantial changes to the U.S. corporate tax system.[105] The Wyden-Coats proposal would enact a flat corporate tax rate of 24%, while also enhancing expensing allowances for small businesses. The legislation proposes repealing a number of corporate tax expenditures, including the Section 199 production activities deduction, certain incentives for oil and gas, certain inventory accounting methods, and depreciation of equipment in excess of the alternative depreciation system, among others.

The Wyden-Coats bill also proposes a number of changes to the U.S. international tax system. Specifically, this legislation would increase taxation of foreign source income—eliminating both

---

[101] Foreign tax credits would be allowed for any taxes paid to a host country.

[102] In supporting documentation, it was noted that the shift to a territorial tax system would be one component of broader tax reform. For more information, see http://waysandmeans.house.gov/UploadedFiles/Summary_of_Ways_and_Means_Draft_Option.pdf. All documents related to this proposal, including the draft legislative text, can be found at http://waysandmeans.house.gov/taxreform/.

[103] See the "Summary of Ways and Means Discussion Draft: Participation Exemption (Territorial) System," available at http://waysandmeans.house.gov/taxreform/.

[104] For more information on territorial tax systems and Chairman Camp's proposal, see CRS Report R42624, *Moving to a Territorial Income Tax: Options and Challenges*, by Jane G. Gravelle.

[105] Several other proposals for fundamental tax reform have been introduced in the 112th Congress. For more information, see CRS Report R41591, *Tax Reform: An Overview of Proposals in the 112th Congress*, by James M. Bickley.

deferral of active foreign earnings while enacting per country foreign tax credit limits.[106] Thus, the Wyden-Coats bill would move the United States' international tax system more in the direction of a worldwide system.

In December 2010, the National Commission of Fiscal Responsibility and Reform (also known as the Fiscal Commission or Simpson-Bowles) released a report outlining a plan for achieving long-run fiscal sustainability. Tax reform was one part of this comprehensive proposal. This Fiscal Commission's illustrative plan recommended reducing the corporate tax rate to 28%, eliminating corporate tax expenditures, including the Section 199 production activities deduction. The plan also proposed moving to a territorial tax system, continuing to tax passive foreign source income under Subpart F. Details on the specific structure of this territorial tax system were not provided.

There are some areas of general consensus with respect to goal of corporate tax reform. Each of the four corporate tax reform proposals summarized in **Table 5** would reduce statutory corporate tax rates (currently at 35%). Part of the revenue cost of rate reduction would be offset by eliminating corporate tax expenditures (which corporate tax expenditures should be eliminated is not an area of broad agreement). There is also general agreement that changes should be made to the current treatment of foreign-source income. There is not, however, a consensus on how a reformed corporate tax system should treat foreign-source income.

One of the most fundamental differences in the corporate tax reform proposals surveyed in **Table 5** is in the proposed treatment of foreign-source income. Both Chairman Camp's and the Fiscal Commission's proposals would move towards a territorial tax system, effectively exempting income earned abroad from U.S. taxation. The Obama Administration's and the Wyden-Coats' proposals both contain provisions that would strengthen the current worldwide system of foreign-source income taxation, reducing the ability for U.S. companies to avoid U.S. taxation through overseas operations.

---

[106] For additional information, see CRS Report R42624, *Moving to a Territorial Income Tax: Options and Challenges*, by Jane G. Gravelle.

The Corporate Income Tax System: Overview and Options for Reform

Table 5. Comparing Business and Corporate Tax Reform Proposals

	Current Law	President's Proposal (2012)[a]	Representative Camp's Proposal (2011)[b]	Wyden-Coats (2011)[c]	Simpson-Bowles (2010)[d]
Top Statutory Corporate Tax Rates	35%	28%	25%	24%	28%
Corporate Tax Expenditures	Dozens of corporate tax expenditure provisions; Total value of $159 billion in 2011	See below	Not explicitly addressed[e]	See below	See below
Provisions to Eliminate Tax Expenditures (Base-Broadening)		Last-in, first-out (LIFO) inventory accounting methods; incentives for oil, gas, and coal; special depreciation for corporate aircraft; reduce interest deductibility		Last-in, first-out (LIFO) inventory accounting methods; Section 199 production activities deduction; certain incentives related to oil and gas; reduce interest deductibility by indexing for inflation[f]	Eliminate most corporate tax expenditures
Provisions to Modify or Add Tax Expenditures		Expand Section 199 domestic production deduction; make R&D tax credit permanent; enhanced incentives for small businesses (cash accounting, increased start-up cost deduction, health insurance tax credit)			
Cost Recovery	Costs recovered under the Modified Accelerated Cost Recovery System (MACRS); 50% bonus depreciation in 2012; $125,000 expensing allowance in 2012	Changes to depreciation rules may be used to broaden corporate tax base; allow small businesses to expense $1 million in investments	Not explicitly addressed[e]	Unlimited expensing for businesses with gross receipts of $1 million or less; depreciation allowances generally limited to accelerated depreciation	Accelerated depreciation eliminated or modified (details not specified)

The Corporate Income Tax System: Overview and Options for Reform

	Current Law	President's Proposal (2012)[a]	Representative Camp's Proposal (2011)[b]	Wyden-Coats (2011)[c]	Simpson-Bowles (2010)[d]
International Taxation	Worldwide tax system with foreign tax credit, deferral, and subpart F	Impose minimum tax on foreign profits with foreign tax credits; provide 20% tax credit for expenses associated with relocating to the U.S.; enhance transfer pricing rules; delay interest expense on foreign earnings until repatriation	Adopt a territorial tax system that exempts 95% of active foreign earnings of a U.S. company's controlled foreign corporation; require U.S. multinationals to pay 5.25% on all pre-existing earnings reinvested abroad (allowing for a foreign tax credit); enhance transfer pricing rules	Tax income on a worldwide basis but end deferral; allow foreign tax credits on a per-country basis; allow a deduction for earnings received from a foreign subsidiary that are reinvested domestically in 2011	Adopt a territorial tax system that exempts most or all of U.S. offshore earnings
Investment Income	Long-term capital gains and dividends taxed at a top rate of 15% in 2012	Tax carried interest as ordinary income[g]	Not explicitly addressed[e]	Tax capital gains and dividends as ordinary income; exclude 35% of certain dividend and capital gain income from gross income	Tax capital gains and dividends as ordinary income

Source: CRS analysis of various tax reform plans and proposals. A brief comparison of business tax reform plans is also provided in Matthew Caminiti and Elizabeth Karasmeighan, *Comparing Business Tax Overhaul Plans*, Bloomberg Government, Washington, DC, 2012.

Notes:

a. The White House and the Department of the Treasury, *The President's Framework for Business Tax Reform*, Washington, DC, February 2012, http://www.treasury.gov/resource-center/tax-policy/Documents/The-Presidents-Framework-for-Business-Tax-Reform-02-22-2012.pdf.

b. The House Ways and Means Committee discussion draft was released on October 26, 2011. The full text of the discussion draft, as well as supporting documentation, can be found at http://waysandmeans.house.gov/taxreform/.

c. The Bipartisan Tax Fairness and Simplification Act of 2011 (S. 727).

d. The National Commission on Fiscal Responsibility and Reform, *The Moment of Truth*, Washington, DC, December 2010, http://www.fiscalcommission.gov/sites/fiscalcommission.gov/files/documents/TheMomentofTruth12_1_2010.pdf.

e. Representative Camp's proposal involves a discussion draft for international tax reform, that could be enacted as part of a broader tax reform designed to reduce the corporate tax rate to 25%. Specifics regarding base-broadening measures and other reforms that would accompany the proposed rate reduction may be released as part of future discussion drafts.

f. A list of tax expenditures that would be repealed as part of the Wyden-Coats proposal can be found at http://www.wyden.senate.gov/imo/media/doc/Offsets%20handout.pdf.

g. The Obama Administration has elsewhere proposed to tax long-term capital gains at 20% and dividends as ordinary income for high-income taxpayers. See Department of the Treasury, *General Explanations of the Administration's Fiscal Year 2013 Revenue Proposals*, Washington, DC, February 2012.

Author Contact Information

Mark P. Keightley
Specialist in Economics
mkeightley@crs.loc.gov, 7-1049

Molly F. Sherlock
Specialist in Public Finance
msherlock@crs.loc.gov, 7-7797

www.ingramcontent.com/pod-product-compliance
Lightning Source LLC
Chambersburg PA
CBHW081244180526
45171CB00005B/539